LITTLE ROCK GIRL 1957

HOW A PHOTOGRAPH CHANGED THE FIGHT FOR INTEGRATION

by Shelley Tougas

Content Adviser: John A. Kirk, PhD,
Chair and Donaghey Professor of History,
History Department, University of Arkansas at Little Rock

COMPASS POINT BOOKS
a capstone imprint

Compass Point Books
1710 Roe Crest Drive
North Mankato, MN 56003

Managing Editor: Catherine Neitge
Designer: Tracy Davies McCabe
Media Researcher: Wanda Winch
Library Consultant: Kathleen Baxter
Production Specialist: Danielle Ceminsky

Image Credits

AP Images: Brian Chilson, 54, Danny Johnston, 52; *Arkansas Democrat Gazette*, 29, 35; Corbis: Bettmann, 17, 19, 21, 26, 27, 47; Courtesy Birmingham Public Library Archives, Cat. 829.1.1.62, 51; Courtesy of the Encyclopedia of Arkansas History & Culture/Photo by Mike Keckhaver, 53; Courtesy of the National Park Service, Little Rock Central High School National Historic Site, 8; Courtesy Women's Emergency Committee to Open Our Schools and Morning Star Studio, 13; Getty Images Inc: Time Life Pictures/Francis Miller, 9, Time Life Pictures/George Silk, 20, Time Life Pictures/Grey Villet, 11; Library of Congress: Prints and Photographs Division, 14, 16, 23, 24, 40, 41, 42, 46, 49, 56 (all), 57 (all), 58, 59; Newscom: Joyce Naltchayan, 33, Steve Keesee, 34; Schomburg Center for Research in Black Culture: Manuscripts, Archives and Rare Book Division, 39; Will Counts Collection: Indiana University Archives, cover, 5, 6, 30, 32, 37, 43, 45

Library of Congress Cataloging-in-Publication Data
Tougas, Shelley.
Little Rock girl 1957: how a photograph changed the fight for integration /
by Shelley Tougas.
   p. cm.—(Captured history)
 Includes bibliographical references and index.
 ISBN 978-0-7565-4440-9 (library binding)
 ISBN 978-0-7565-4512-3 (paperback)
 1. School integration—Arkansas—Little Rock—Juvenile literature. 2. Central High
School (Little Rock, Ark.)—Juvenile literature. 3. African American high school
students—Arkansas—Little Rock—Juvenile literature. 4. Little Rock (Ark.)—Race
relations—Juvenile literature. 5. Eckford, Elizabeth, 1942—Juvenile literature.
I. Title. II. Series.
LC214.23.L56T68 2012
379.2′630976773—dc22   2010054303

Visit Compass Point Books on the Internet at *www.capstonepub.com*

Printed in the United States of America in North Mankato, Minnesota.
022013   007194R

TABLE**OF**CONTENTS

Chapter One

CRISIS IN LITTLE ROCK

The crowd erupted angrily when 15-year-old Elizabeth Eckford neared Little Rock Central High School. Television equipment recorded their jeering: "Two, four, six, eight—we don't want to integrate!"

Elizabeth squeezed her books against her freshly ironed shirtwaist dress and walked toward the school door. Sunglasses hid the fear in her eyes as she looked around. *Where are the others?* she wondered.

Nine African-American teenagers, who would forever be known as the Little Rock Nine, were supposed to arrive at the all-white high school on September 4, 1957, and make history together. From the students who had applied, school officials had handpicked the nine teenagers to become the school's first African-American students.

But at that moment, Elizabeth was all alone. A mob of angry white people, several hundred in all, followed her to the entrance to the high school.

"Go back to where you came from!" a woman shouted at her.

Elizabeth had felt a moment of hope when she noticed soldiers with rifles near the school's entrance. She guessed that the soldiers' job was to make sure she and the eight other students entered the school safely.

Elizabeth guessed wrong.

"Two, four, six, eight—we don't want to integrate!"

A white student passes through a line of National Guardsmen as they block Elizabeth Eckford's entrance to Little Rock Central High School.

As she approached the door, the soldiers, who were in the Arkansas National Guard, crossed their rifles and blocked her path. On the orders of Arkansas' governor, Orval Faubus, they wouldn't allow her to enter the building. Her legs started shaking. The crowd continued to yell. "Go home! Whites have rights too!"

She looked for a calm adult, someone who would make her feel safe. She noticed a woman with a kind face, but the woman lunged forward and spit on her.

Elizabeth held back tears. She didn't know what to do. Photographers and reporters circled her and the crowd, recording every movement.

Elizabeth spun around and started walking wordlessly back toward the street. A white teenager, Hazel Bryan, walked behind her. Hazel normally had a bright smile to match her perky brown curls. But at that moment her face twisted with rage. "Go home, nigger!" she screamed. "Go back to Africa!"

Photographer Will Counts of the local newspaper, the *Arkansas Democrat*, snapped a photo and sealed the

Photographer Will Counts said when he "saw Hazel Bryan's contorted face in the camera's viewfinder, I knew that I had released the shutter at an important moment."

image in American history: Elizabeth, hoping to get the same education that her white peers were getting, and Hazel, determined to keep her from getting it. Counts' photo, and others from the Little Rock conflict, revealed a divided nation. The Civil War had ended nearly 100 years earlier, but the country's hostilities clearly had not disappeared.

Unable to get into school, Elizabeth sat on a bench at a bus stop. The crowd followed with name-calling and threats. Somebody urged the others to drag Elizabeth to a tree and hang her.

"It's one of these almost incredible things, to see normal people, many of them—most of them—churchgoers, and if you'd get them in their homes, they would be the kindest, nicest people," said Benjamin Fine, a New York newspaper reporter who had been sent to Little Rock to cover the story. "But in a mob group, something happens when that group gets together."

Three reporters formed a protective ring around Elizabeth to keep the crowd from getting close. She sat motionless on the bench, waiting for a bus to take her away. Fine, of *The New York Times*, slid next to Elizabeth and put his arm around her. People in the crowd were shocked. White men in the South simply did not behave this way. Fine's action most likely made him a target for the mob during his stay in Little Rock. "Individually they would be nice to me, but in the group they would be ready, if they could, to tear me limb from limb. Many times they would just come up and bang me in the back or trip me or step on my foot or do all kinds of annoyances. By the end of the day I was black and blue," he said.

Fine comforted Elizabeth. "Don't let them see you cry," he told her.

Another reporter peppered Elizabeth with questions. "Can you tell me your name, please? Are you going to go to school here at Central High? You don't care to say anything, is that right?" Elizabeth didn't answer.

Grace Lorch, a white woman who was a longtime civil rights supporter, came to Elizabeth's aid. "She's just a little girl!"

"Don't let them see you cry."

Grace Lorch (left) kept back the mob that surrounded Elizabeth Eckford as she waited at a bus stop bench after being denied entrance to Central High School.

National Guard troops kept other members of the Little Rock Nine from entering Central High School.

she scolded the crowd. The woman boarded the bus with Elizabeth and helped calm the terrified teenager.

By the time Elizabeth had reached the bus stop, the eight other African-American students had also been turned away from the school by the soldiers. The parents of the eight students had received phone calls the night before with instructions from Daisy Bates, president of the Arkansas chapter of the National Association for the Advancement of Colored People (NAACP). They were to meet the next morning, and a handful of ministers, both black and white, would walk with the students to school to help them feel safe. The ministers also would serve to remind the hostile crowd of the importance of tolerance.

Elizabeth's family never got a phone call explaining the plan for the Little Rock Nine. They didn't have a telephone. Elizabeth had boarded the bus and later faced the taunts, name-calling, and hatred alone. She may have felt abandoned. But a camera clicked, and soon the world was watching. It would witness her courage and that of the other eight students.

"From the time Elizabeth first approached the National Guard, you knew this was a major confrontation between the governor and the federal government," Counts said later about his famous photograph. "She became a symbol for the Little Rock crisis."

"She became a symbol for the Little Rock crisis."

COURAGEOUS CIVIL RIGHTS LEADER

A note attached to a rock thrown through a window of the home of civil rights leader Daisy Gatson Bates read: "Stone this time. Dynamite next."

In a white man's world, Daisy Gatson Bates, an African-American woman, was a rare leader. Bates and her husband, L.C. Bates, ran a newspaper that supported and chronicled the civil rights movement. In 1952 Bates became president of the Arkansas chapter of the NAACP. Her role thrust her into the spotlight during segregation battles, including the confrontation in Little Rock.

As an adviser to the Little Rock Nine, Bates let her home become the headquarters for civil rights leaders during the confrontation. She and her husband received countless threats and suffered numerous attacks because of their work. Pressure from segregationists made them lose advertising and forced them to close their newspaper, the *Arkansas State Press,* in 1959.

Bates was known for showing remarkable courage. She once insisted that a white attorney call her "Mrs. Bates" instead of "Daisy," an unthinkable challenge of white power. The Associated Press chose her as the Woman of the Year in Education in 1957. She was also named one of the top 10 newsmakers in the world.

Bates' childhood was marked by tragedy. Three white men murdered her mother, and her father abandoned her. Friends of her family raised her. After the confrontation in Little Rock, Bates worked in Washington, D.C., ran community programs in Arkansas, wrote a book, and briefly revived the family newspaper. She died in 1999. Little Rock honored Bates' contributions by naming an elementary school after her as well as a street that passes Little Rock Central High School. Arkansas celebrates a state holiday in her honor.

Chapter Two

QUEST FOR EQUAL RIGHTS

Segregation was the law of the land in the South in the decades following Reconstruction after the Civil War. Under Jim Crow laws, as they were called, African-Americans and whites were separated in schools, parks, theaters, and buses, and at lunch counters, drinking fountains, and other places. Blacks who violated segregation laws could be arrested or worse. Angry mobs were known to harass, beat, and even kill African-Americans who dared to enter whites-only territory.

Jim Crow laws stayed on the books even in communities with large groups of African-Americans. White citizens could change laws by electing new leaders. But Jim Crow laws created voting barriers for African-Americans. It was difficult, if not impossible, for them to change this situation through elections because most African-Americans could not vote.

Still, African-Americans organized through groups such as the NAACP and the Southern Christian Leadership Conference. The groups challenged segregation by filing lawsuits in courts and by protesting publicly.

When Elizabeth Eckford confronted the angry mob at Little Rock Central High School in 1957, the fight for equal rights was well under way.

In 1947 Jackie Robinson had become the first African-American to play major league baseball since the 1800s.

Angry mobs were known to harass, beat, and even kill African-Americans who dared to enter whites-only territory.

DO YOU WANT NEGROES IN OUR SCHOOLS?

IF YOU DO NOT THEN GO TO THE POLLS THIS COMING MONDAY AND

VOTE

FOR REMOVAL | AGAINST REMOVAL

LAMB | McKINLEY
MATSON | ROWLAND
TUCKER | LASTER

THIS IS THE SIMPLE TRUTH. IF THE INTEGRATIONISTS WIN THIS SCHOOL BOARD FIGHT, THE SCHOOLS WILL BE INTEGRATED THIS FALL. THERE WILL BE ABSOLUTELY NOTHING YOU OR WE CAN DO TO STOP IT.

PLEASE VOTE RIGHT!!!

Join hands with us in this fight— send your contributions to

THE MOTHERS' LEAGUE

P. O. BOX 3321 • LITTLE ROCK, ARKANSAS

Ad Paid for by Margaret C. Jackson, President; Mary Thomason, Secretary

Most of the members of the segregationist Mothers' League were not mothers of Central High School students.

President Dwight D. Eisenhower banned discrimination in federal jobs in 1953. And police in Montgomery, Alabama, arrested Rosa Parks in 1955 for refusing to give her bus seat to a white passenger. The arrest prompted a black boycott, which forced city leaders to integrate buses.

Known as a progressive small city, Little Rock didn't seem an obvious battleground in the conflict over equal access to public schools. The city was not part of the Deep South, where racial tensions had erupted repeatedly since slavery was outlawed in 1865. The University of Arkansas had become the first traditional southern university to integrate when it enrolled a black student in its law school in 1948. And Little Rock's buses and libraries had been desegregated without conflict.

The spark that ignited the Little Rock conflict came from the United States Supreme Court. The court ruled in 1954 that segregation in public schools was unconstitutional. Until the ruling, in a case called *Brown v. Board of Education*, segregation had been allowed under a practice known as "separate but equal." The thinking was that if a separate park, school, or hospital for African-Americans was just as good as a park, school, or hospital for whites, that was acceptable.

In May 1954, on the steps of the U.S. Supreme Court, Nettie Hunt explained to her daughter Nikie the importance of the *Brown v. Board of Education* decision.

> "Equal means getting the same thing, at the same time, and in the same place."

In reality the facilities for African-Americans were never as good. Thurgood Marshall, the African-American attorney who argued the case before the Supreme Court, explained why separate was *not* equal. "Equal means getting the same thing, at the same time, and in the same place," he said. In the *Brown* case, the court agreed with Marshall. It said school segregation stripped African-American students of educational opportunities and harmed them emotionally.

One hundred and one southern members of Congress who supported segregation vowed to oppose *Brown*. In a written statement, titled the *Southern Manifesto*, they said they had the "gravest concern for the explosive and dangerous condition created by this decision ... ."

What happened in Little Rock was not just a battle about whether African-Americans could enter one school. The conflict tested the federal government's authority over state and local government. The Little Rock School Board already had approved a watered-down plan to bring black students into white schools. The plan could not be considered bold. It called for gradually enrolling African-American students over a number of years.

Yet segregationists refused to let the plan unfold.

Governor Orval Faubus sent the state's National Guard troops to prevent the students from entering the school. He claimed he was trying to protect the Little Rock Nine and prevent violence. But his action—and his words—made the situation worse. If African-Americans tried to enroll, he predicted, there would be "violence and bloodshed."

A LEGAL WARRIOR

Thurgood Marshall, the first African-American Supreme Court justice, was the grandson of a slave.

Some African-American leaders fought for civil rights with political protests. Others stood at the pulpit in churches and used religion to make their case. Thurgood Marshall was a warrior in the courtroom.

Marshall, who was born in Baltimore, Maryland, wanted to attend the University of Maryland School of Law. But he learned that the school's segregation policy would prevent his admission. So Marshall earned a law degree at Howard University School of Law instead. He later sued the University of Maryland for its segregation policies. He won. In an interesting twist of fate, the university's law library is now called the Thurgood Marshall Law Library.

Known as "the little man's lawyer," Marshall built a reputation by fighting—and winning—many civil rights cases. A lot of his clients couldn't afford to pay him. But Marshall cared more about making a difference than building a bank account.

He was chief counsel for the NAACP's Legal Defense and Educational Fund. Among his most famous cases is *Brown v. Board of Education*. Nearly 60 years after the Supreme Court had allowed the legal separation of African-Americans and whites, Marshall and others challenged the idea of "separate but equal" schools.

The court agreed that separate was not equal. Slowly, schools, parks, buses, and other public places began to be integrated. In 1961 President John F. Kennedy appointed Marshall to serve on a federal appeals court. Six years later President Lyndon Johnson appointed Marshall to the U.S. Supreme Court, making him the first African-American to serve on the country's highest court.

Marshall became a larger-than-life figure, speaking bluntly about legal issues, race, and politics. He retired from the court in 1991 and died two years later.

Daisy Bates, the African-American leader who advised the Little Rock Nine and their families, wrote later that "hysteria in all of its madness enveloped the city. Racial feelings were at a fever pitch."

For more than two weeks after the students were barred from entering Central High School, politicians and lawyers argued about what should happen next. Citizens protested. White students went to school. And the Little Rock Nine stayed home.

Members of the Little Rock Nine studied together when they were barred from school.

A federal judge ordered Governor Faubus to allow the Little Rock Nine to begin school. A date was set: September 23, 1957. Bates set a second plan in motion. The students were to gather at her home and go to school as a group.

This time they were able to get inside the school. The attention of an angry mob was focused on a group of African-American reporters. Several people assaulted the newsmen. A reporter from Memphis, L. Alex Wilson, was hit over the head with a brick.

When the crowd realized that the students had slipped inside unnoticed, they threatened to riot. The Little Rock Nine had to flee school grounds for their safety.

The chaos at Little Rock was not just a state news story, or even a national news story. The photograph of Elizabeth Eckford and the angry mob, and news stories about the event, had circled the globe. The fact that a state governor was ignoring federal orders made people around the world wonder whether, as Faubus warned, the situation would turn into a bloodbath.

Many of Little Rock's white residents refused to support the governor and segregationists. They objected to the governor's actions and called for a citywide prayer service. Little Rock Mayor Woodrow Mann asked the federal government to ensure that Central High was integrated peacefully.

President Dwight D. Eisenhower finally listened. He went on national television and announced his plans.

The photograph of Elizabeth Eckford and the angry mob, and news stories about the event, had circled the globe.

Members of the 101st Airborne Division forced segregationist protesters away from Central High School at bayonet point.

He decided to send the 101st Airborne Division to enforce the federal court's order. He also federalized the Arkansas National Guard, which meant that the president, not the Arkansas governor, was now its commander.

With all the paratroopers and the National Guard soldiers, Little Rock resembled a war zone. But the strategy worked. The mob broke up, and on September 25 the Little Rock Nine finally entered school—and stayed.

Some of Central High's white students wanted to show the world they were not bigots. "This is the chance that

Federal troops protected members of the Little Rock Nine as they walked into school, but they could not be with them every minute.

the youth of America has been waiting for," student Jane Emery wrote in the Central High student newspaper, *The Tiger*. "Through an open mind, broad outlook, wise thinking, and a careful choice you can prove that America's youth has not 'gone to the dogs,' that their moral, spiritual, and educational standards are not being lowered. This is the opportunity for you as citizens of Arkansas and students of Little Rock Central High to show the world that Arkansas is a progressive thriving state of wide-awake alert people."

Elizabeth Eckford and other members of the Little Rock Nine were always on their guard—at lunch, in the gym, in the halls, and during class.

But the students' good intentions were not enough. The conflict simply moved out of sight of the troops. For the Little Rock Nine, school days weren't filled with happy yearbook memories. Every day a group of white students, fewer than 100 in total, tormented the Little Rock Nine. The bullies shoved them in the halls. They spat on them. They threw sharp pencils at them.

No place was safe. In gym class the bullies scalded the Little Rock Nine in the locker room showers. At lunch they threw food at them. White students who defended the black students were threatened and bullied too. Most students just looked the other way. So did many teachers.

"People around me that I saw didn't react to what they saw or what they had to have heard," Elizabeth said later. "They turned their backs. It was impossible to have a friend. This was not anything like a normal environment. Anybody that would talk to us got a lot of pressure."

Then the attacks turned dangerous. A white student sprayed acid into Melba Pattillo's eyes. Yet she refused to give up. She continued to come to school. "I had to become a warrior," she told CNN years later. "I had to learn not how to dress the best but how to get from that door to the end of the hall without dying."

Finally one of the Little Rock Nine could no longer handle the abuse. Minnijean Brown dumped a bowl of chili on a boy who blocked her way. She was suspended from school and, after more confrontation, she was expelled.

Outside of school the conflict returned to the courtroom. The school board, which had been open to gradual desegregation, lost some of its moderate members in elections. Segregationists gained control of the board. The new board asked the court to delay integration. One court agreed, but the U.S. Supreme Court ordered that integration be continued.

Governor Faubus was determined to defy the federal government. Since he couldn't prevent African-Americans from attending school with whites, he decided to close Little Rock's high schools. Then he called for

"I had to become a warrior. I had to learn not how to dress the best but how to get from that door to the end of the hall without dying."

a referendum. Voters would be asked whether they supported or opposed school integration.

Jefferson Thomas, one of the Little Rock Nine, was stunned by the news that school would not reopen in the fall. "After the governor closed the schools," he said later, "I knew I was in the right place. That the governor would say, 'To stop a few black kids from getting an education, I'm going to deny it to 2,000 whites' is amazing."

In September 1958 Little Rock citizens voted 19,470 to 7,561 to oppose integration. The schools remained closed.

Four Central High School students read a misspelled sign near their school. Little Rock high schools were closed by the governor, not the federal government.

THIS SCHOOL CLOSED BY ORDER OF THE FEDERAL GOVERMENT

THE MAN BEHIND THE CONFLICT

Six-term governor Orval Faubus was considered the "most loved" and "most hated" politician in Arkansas.

Governor Orval E. Faubus was a man of surprises. He did not oppose the integration of public transportation in Arkansas. But a short time later, he *did* oppose the integration of Little Rock Central High School. He supported programs that expanded the power of the federal government. But he *opposed* the federal government's using its power in his state. First elected in 1954, Faubus was considered a moderate politician when it came to issues of race. Some of his supporters were surprised, then, that he used the National Guard to keep African-Americans from attending Central High School. He claimed he was trying to prevent violence.

President Dwight D. Eisenhower personally talked to Faubus. The president hoped Faubus would change his mind and follow a federal court order. Faubus refused, so Eisenhower sent in troops, and the Little

Rock Nine were finally able to enter the building. Observers say Faubus was afraid that segregationists would ruin his re-election chances if he didn't fight integration. Whatever the reason, he won political points in Arkansas for standing up to the federal government. In 1958 a national survey found that Faubus was among the "Ten Men in the World Most Admired by Americans."

Though Faubus served as governor for 12 years, he did not seek re-election to a seventh term in 1966. Ten years before his death, Faubus pulled another surprise. He supported Jesse Jackson, an African-American, in Jackson's failed bid to become the 1984 Democratic presidential candidate. Faubus praised Jackson, saying that "he speaks out for the underdogs of the nation."

For an entire year, every high school student in Little Rock had to find another schooling option. Some enrolled in private schools, some moved away or traveled to other public school districts, and some took correspondence courses.

Segregationists on the school board, meanwhile, punished teachers and administrators who supported integration by attempting to fire 44 of them.

Other community leaders had had enough of the conflict. They organized and persuaded new people to run for the school board. They wanted board members who would support an integration plan and show the world that Little Rock could move forward.

And that's exactly what happened. Three new school board members took office, and the board announced plans to open the high schools early. Segregationists protested, but only briefly. Police arrested nearly two dozen protesters and broke up the mob—this time for good.

It appeared that integration was finally real, but once again, the step forward was a small one. After a year of political and legal battles, only two of the Little Rock Nine came back to Central High School. The others had moved, decided to attend other schools, or received diplomas through correspondence courses.

Elizabeth Eckford never returned to Central after that first horrible year. She accumulated enough credits to graduate by taking courses elsewhere.

Ernest Green, the only senior among the Little Rock Nine, became the first African-American to graduate from Central High School. He graduated in May 1958, the spring before Little Rock residents voted against integration and to keep the schools closed.

It took many years to fully integrate Little Rock's public schools, and court battles continue today. President Bill Clinton, a former Arkansas governor, honored the Little Rock Nine in 1999 for their bravery. Each received the Congressional Gold Medal, the nation's highest civilian award.

Ernest Green went on to receive degrees from Michigan State University after graduating from Central High School.

Another view of Hazel Bryan's heckling was selected by *Life* magazine as one of "100 photographs that changed the world." It was taken by a United Press photographer.

Chapter Three

TWO SYMBOLIC PHOTOS

When the crisis erupted at Little Rock Central High School, newspaper photographer Will Counts had an edge. He was a hometown boy, born and raised in Arkansas. Even more important: He was a former Central High student. Only about a decade before, he'd discovered his passion for photography in the same school that was later surrounded by soldiers.

Counts put both his passion and hometown knowledge to use September 4, 1957. He knew the layout of the campus. That morning he dressed in an everyday plaid shirt for work. He planned to blend in with the crowd, unlike the suit-and-tie newsmen from the big cities. And unlike many of the photographers, who hoped to take their time and get one perfect shot, Counts had a different strategy. He figured the more photos he shot, the more likely he'd get the ideal photograph. It was a matter of improving his odds.

Counts also used a small camera, one that didn't draw attention like the large professional cameras used by other photographers. He could shoot 36 exposures with his 35mm Nikon S2 before he had to reload, a huge advantage over the other photographers, who had to reload their Speed Graphic cameras after every shot. The small camera let him slip through crowds and get close to the action.

"While other photographers were content with

"While other photographers were content with capturing your average newspaper photo ... young Counts was always where the action was."

Photographer Will Counts and his small 35mm camera were front and center during the Little Rock crisis.

capturing your average newspaper photo—people milling around the high school, soldiers standing guard—young Counts was always where the action was: People were marching and screaming and protesting. They were on the move, and Counts was right in front of them," said an article in *The Arkansas Leader* published after his death in 2001.

When the crowd of protesters confronted Elizabeth Eckford with threats and jeers, Counts was ready. He managed to get in front of the crowd. He had a wide-angle lens to get the shot he wanted: Elizabeth against a backdrop of angry people. But the crowd kept pressing forward, making it difficult for Counts to get *any* pictures, let alone a good one. He had to run backward awkwardly, trying to avoid tripping, to stay in front of the mob.

Click. Click. Click. Counts had snapped a high-quality, technically sound picture. That much he knew. But Counts

Elizabeth Eckford's stoic expression was in sharp contrast to Hazel Bryan's snarling face.

> "For him, it was community journalism, even though it was a national story."

had no idea that a single photograph would become a magnifying glass for race relations in the United States.

"For him, it was community journalism, even though it was a national story," said Jim Kelly, an Indiana University professor who knew Counts. "He wasn't there as a stranger. I don't know that he knew those two women, but he knew the situation. He knew what it was like to go to a segregated school."

The photo helped build his career. The Associated Press named it one of the top 100 photographs of the 20th century. Counts was nominated for the Pulitzer Prize, the highest award in American journalism, for photographs he took during the Central High conflict.

Counts took another photo later that also made international news. L. Alex Wilson, an African-American journalist, was attacked outside Central High by a man wielding a brick. Counts snapped a photo, and the image of Wilson's beating is among those that prompted national leaders to take action. Years later the photo was selected by Encyclopaedia Britannica as one of the world's 50 most memorable news photos of the preceding 50 years.

Counts took a different path with his photography after the conflict at Central High. After working as a photographer for the Associated Press, he joined the journalism faculty at Indiana University, where he earned a PhD. During his 32 years of teaching at Indiana, Counts said, he used the Little Rock photos in just about every course. "I always cited them as evidence of the power

Counts' photo of L. Alex Wilson being brutally attacked is said to have prompted President Dwight D. Eisenhower to send troops to Little Rock.

of the image to communicate the news. I have always believed that good news reporting (both pictures *and* words) did make a difference in Little Rock."

Counts kept his students focused on the essentials of photojournalism, said Kelly. "For you to do less than your best was a breach of the trust that subjects were placing in you," he said Counts told his students. "It was always about journalism. We'd talk about cameras, lenses and film, but it was primarily about getting the story right."

Through the years Counts never stopped thinking about Elizabeth Eckford and Hazel Bryan. His most famous work would be the photos of the conflict in Little Rock, and of the reconciliation of the two women many years later. He documented their meeting in the book *A Life Is More Than a Moment: The Desegregation of Little Rock's Central High.*

On the 40th anniversary of the Little Rock crisis, a reconciliation celebration was planned to show the world that Little Rock's citizens had moved forward peacefully and had learned to cooperate and accept one another. President Bill Clinton would hold open the school doors while the nine former students, now adults, entered Central High School.

President Bill Clinton opened the Central High School door for Carlotta Walls LaNier and the rest of the Little Rock Nine in 1997.

CENTRAL HIGH SCHOOL

Counts would be there in 1997. In a powerful symbol of change, Counts would again photograph the two women from his famous picture. But this time the image would represent a hopeful future rather than a shameful past.

Counts did not know that six years after the conflict, Hazel Bryan Massery had called Elizabeth Eckford to apologize for her behavior. Hazel was afraid a single photograph had forever cast her as a hateful racist. She believed she had been too young in 1957 to truly have her own beliefs. In those difficult times, Hazel told people, she had reflected the beliefs of her family, friends, and community.

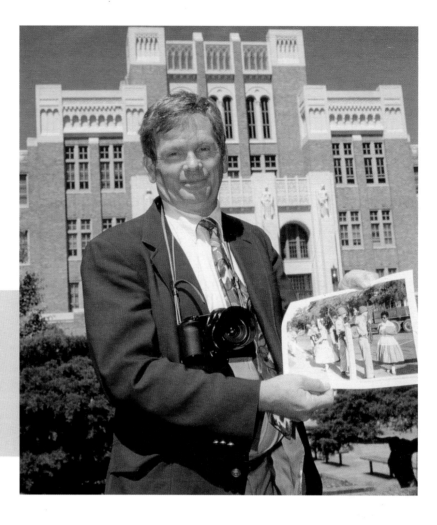

"I knew that my life was more than a moment."

With a few phone calls in 1997, Counts asked the women to meet. Massery, now a grandmother, was eager to shed the image created by the photo. "I knew that my life was more than a moment," she said.

Counts was not sure Eckford would agree to the meeting. A shy child and a quiet woman, she had never embraced her role as a face of the civil rights movement. She typically had refused media interviews and speaking requests. But to his surprise, Eckford, who lives in Little Rock, told Counts she would participate.

Forty years after they had made world news, the women came together for a new photograph at Central High School. They talked. They put their arms around each other. They smiled for the camera. And Counts snapped another photo.

The photo appears on a poster titled *Reconciliation* with the original photo in a corner. Sold at the visitor's center near the school, each poster has a sticker with a quote from Eckford: "True reconciliation can occur only when we honestly acknowledge our painful, but shared, past."

Something else happened as the camera clicked: Seeds for a relationship were planted. Elizabeth and Hazel became friends. Soon they began speaking publicly about the past that haunted them both. They met with reporters and spoke to groups about the conflict. They considered writing a book, and they appeared together on *The Oprah Winfrey Show*.

The women's friends and family members thought the relationship was odd and perhaps forced. Some people accused Massery of seeking the media attention that Eckford had spent a lifetime avoiding. Other members of the Little Rock Nine weren't sure what to think.

"We kind of joked about it," Ernest Green said. "Here she is, framed forever with her mouth spewing out whatever she was spewing out, and no matter what she does in life, she can't erase that photo."

Eckford began to have doubts too. She wondered whether Massery was truly sorry. The friendly

Counts' 1997 photo of Elizabeth Eckford and Hazel Bryan Massery at Central High School symbolized reconciliation, not hatred.

relationship did not last, and the women no longer appear in public together.

Counts' widow, Vivian, called the reconciliation photo one of her husband's most cherished works. The meeting Counts helped set up "was an attempt to reconcile, an attempt to heal some of those wounds," she said. "I'm just glad he did not know how things have turned around, and how the wounds have reopened for those two women."

ChapterFour
THE AMERICAN DREAM

Will Counts' photo of Elizabeth Eckford told the story of segregation in an instant. But it did more than tell the facts—it provoked a reaction.

Americans were stunned by the depth of racial hatred suggested by the photo. The twisted, snarling face of Hazel Bryan hinted at racism's deep roots in American culture. In contrast, Elizabeth's resolute appearance in the face of such hostility suggested that African-Americans were determined to use and defend their basic constitutional rights—rights taken for granted by most Americans.

The idea that *every* person should be able to get a basic education, paid for by taxpayers, arose early in the history of the United States. The nation's early leaders agreed that to succeed, a democratic form of government needs educated citizens, so they set up public schools.

Throughout the world, a good education had usually been reserved for a small group of people, typically boys from wealthy white families. In some cultures, girls, members of minority groups, and poor people didn't get formal educations at all. Many lived their whole lives without knowing how to read or write.

But in the United States, public education became a cornerstone of community life. Many white children attended elementary school in the 1800s. Still, only 2 percent of the population in 1870 had finished high school. During

> The twisted, snarling face of Hazel Bryan hinted at racism's deep roots in American culture.

African-Americans had been excluded from public education for years. The 1839 *Anti-Slavery Almanac* portrayed black students barred from school.

the ensuing years, high school graduation rates soared. Graduation became the ticket to a decent job and entry into the growing American middle class.

The country's success with public education didn't cross racial lines, though. Far fewer African-Americans than whites finished high school. And their schools were different from white schools. Blacks' "separate but equal" schools were far from equal.

In Little Rock, for example, Central High School, built in 1927 at a cost of $1.5 million, was considered state-of-the-art. The city's high school for African-American students was built two years later for $400,000, only about one-fourth the cost of the white high school. But Dunbar High School was considered one of the best

A teacher and 75 sixth-graders crowded into a room in an old Muskogee, Oklahoma, store that served as a school for African-Americans in 1917.

African-American high schools in the country. Across the South white students typically had modern school buildings and better equipment and more academic programs than black students did.

Schools for African-Americans were poorly funded. Teachers were paid less. Textbooks were old, and often students had to share supplies because there weren't enough for everyone. Some buildings were in such poor condition that they were unsafe. Buses filled with white students went past African-American neighborhoods and did not stop. Kids in those neighborhoods often had to walk long distances to their schools.

Faced with court challenges, segregationists saw they

One teacher taught all grades in 1941 at a school for African-Americans in Veazy, Georgia.

would lose their cause if they did not spend money to improve African-American schools. But new money did not change the fact that white students went to one school and African-Americans went to another. States and cities had a practical problem as well. Taxpayers had the burden of supporting two separate public school systems. It was too costly.

Most Americans believe that students, no matter how poor, can grow into successful adults if they get a good education and work hard. The United States is portrayed as a melting pot, a place where people of various races, religions, and cultures come together and unite as one nation. All of those people should have an equal chance to succeed, thanks to public schools. It is the American dream.

The photos from Little Rock show students who wanted the American dream so badly that they were willing to confront the military. Elizabeth Eckford's photograph suggested that the American dream was a lie—at least for African-Americans.

Dorothy Butler Gilliam, an African-American reporter, summed up the reaction of millions of Americans to the attempt to integrate schools: "If this is what it takes to bring this about, what kind of country is this?"

Reporters found it difficult to be neutral on the issue. *New York Times* reporter Benjamin Fine had put his arm around Elizabeth to make her feel safe. It was a

Jefferson Thomas, walking with Elizabeth Eckford in 1957, was one of only two African-American students to return to Central after the school was closed for a year. The other was Carlotta Walls.

Reporter Benjamin Fine (wearing a bow tie) became a target of segregationists after he comforted Elizabeth Eckford at the bus stop.

human reaction, but not a professional one. Reporters are not supposed to be part of the story. They aren't supposed to get involved in what they cover.

But the hatred and violence were impossible to ignore. African-American reporters were beaten when they tried to cover the protests. Newsmen heard the threats and saw the violence. Segregationists threatened white reporters, too, but they rarely hurt them seriously.

"We knew what the right side was," said Herb Kaplow, a journalist who covered key moments in the civil rights movement. "America was coming to grips with it, you know. There were things happening before *Brown* [*vs. Board of Education*] and the armed forces were desegregated; things were happening. The American public was coming to see [segregation] for what it was, a terrible institution."

Americans, especially outside the South, were outraged by the treatment of the Little Rock Nine. Many adults believed that the teenage protesters such as the sneering Hazel Bryan were immature and caught up in the moment. Youth and a lack of experience could explain their actions. But the adults in the crowd were another matter. How could adults—parents, neighbors, churchgoers—threaten and harass children who were only trying to get an education?

While segregationists threatened and harassed the Little Rock Nine and their families, others came forward to help. The news coverage motivated people to get

"If this is what it takes to bring this about, what kind of country is this?"

Segregationists rallied at the state Capitol against allowing black students to attend Central High School.

involved. Strangers called and wrote to Elizabeth Eckford, praising her courage. People left gifts of cash at her grandfather's store. Famous people, such as actress and singer Lena Horne and Nobel Peace Prize winner Ralph Bunche, wanted to shake hands with the Little Rock Nine.

Bill Clinton, who was governor of Arkansas before becoming president, was just 11 years old when the Central

In 1959 a mob marched from the Capitol to Central High School to protest integration.

High School crisis erupted. He would later say the Little Rock Nine shaped his views on race and justice.

"It was Little Rock," he said, "that made racial equality a driving obsession in my life."

Civil rights leaders eventually won the conflict at Central High School, but their victory was not the end of

It took federal troops to resolve the Little Rock crisis, but the civil rights movement is far from over.

the movement. They learned important lessons about the power of a single photo. News coverage could change the course of the movement. If they could show Americans the horror of racism, if they could show them the determination of African-Americans to share basic rights, then the nation's leaders would have to respond.

THE REST OF THE LITTLE ROCK NINE

Elizabeth Eckford's picture is forever etched in history: a young girl, her eyes hidden behind sunglasses, tightly holding books as if they could shield her from the rage of the angry mob. Although Eckford became the face of the Little Rock confrontation, eight other students also tried to enter the school that day. Together they are known as the Little Rock Nine. Meet the other eight:

Minnijean Brown Trickey. Like the rest of the Little Rock Nine, Minnijean Brown was constantly tormented at school. She was expelled after calling one of the bullies "white trash." Trickey attended Southern Illinois University before moving with her husband to Canada, where she lived for several years. She received bachelor's and master's degrees in social work from Canadian universities. She is a social activist and college teacher, and she worked in the U.S. Department of the Interior during the Clinton administration.

Ernest Green. The first black student to graduate from Central High, Ernest Green attended Michigan State University, where he received bachelor's and master's degrees. He served as an assistant U.S. secretary of housing and uban affairs in Washington, D.C., and later joined an investment banking firm, where he was a senior managing director. He is retired.

Gloria Ray Karlmark. After graduating from high school in Kansas City, Missouri, Gloria Ray Karlmark attended Illinois Institute of Technology, where she earned a bachelor's degree in chemistry and mathematics. She worked as a systems analyst and technical writer in Sweden before becoming a patent attorney there. She also published an international computer applications journal and worked in the Netherlands. She lives in Europe.

Thelma Mothershed Wair. After earning high school credits by correspondence courses and summer school, Thelma Mothershed received a high school diploma by mail from Central High School. She earned bachelor's and master's degrees from Southern Illinois University and taught home economics in Illinois for 28 years before retiring in 1994. She also volunteered in a program for victims of domestic abuse. She now lives in Little Rock.

Melba Pattillo Beals. The author of two books detailing her experiences in Little Rock and after, Melba Pattillo finished high school in California, where she lived with a sponsoring family from the NAACP. She graduated from San Francisco State University, majoring in journalism, and earned a master's degree from the Columbia University Graduate School of Journalism. She worked for television stations in the San Francisco Bay area before becoming a consultant and motivational speaker. Her first book, *Warriors Don't Cry: A Searing Memoir of the Battle to Integrate Little Rock's Central High School*, was named an American Library Association Notable Book for 1995. Its sequel, *White Is a State of Mind: A Memoir*, was published in 1999. She is chair of the department of communications at Dominican University of California, where she teaches journalism.

Terrence Roberts. The Roberts family moved to California after the historic school year in Little Rock. Terrence Roberts graduated from high school in California and earned bachelor's and master's degrees in California. After earning a doctorate from Southern Illinois University in Carbondale, he taught at the college level. He runs a management consulting firm and works as a psychologist.

Jefferson Thomas. A track athlete, Jefferson Thomas had to give up his sport to attend Central High. School leaders would not allow the Little Rock Nine to participate in extracurricular activities. Thomas received a degree from California State University in Los Angeles. After serving in the Army in Vietnam, Thomas had a career in accounting with Mobil Oil and the U.S. Department of Defense. He died of cancer in 2010.

Carlotta Walls LaNier. The youngest of the Little Rock Nine, Carlotta Walls LaNier attended Michigan State University for two years and graduated from what is now the University of Northern Colorado. She owns a real estate brokerage firm in Denver and is president of the Little Rock Nine Foundation, a scholarship and mentoring organization.

Civil rights leader Daisy Bates with the Little Rock Nine in 1957. They are (front row, from left) Thelma Mothershed, Minnijean Brown, Elizabeth Eckford, Gloria Ray, and (back row, from left) Ernest Green, Melba Pattillo, Terrence Roberts, Carlotta Walls, Bates, and Jefferson Thomas.

After the events in Little Rock, African-Americans across the South tried to enroll in all-white schools. A few schools were integrated peacefully, but most attempts met resistance.

Fred Shuttlesworth, who would become one of the civil rights movement's most important leaders, was attacked when he attempted to enroll his daughters in a Birmingham, Alabama, school in 1957. Shuttlesworth intended to enroll the children in Phillips High School, an all-white school with an excellent reputation. With news cameras present, a group of white men lunged at Shuttlesworth and beat him severely. His wife was stabbed in the hip when she tried to stop the men. Police finally broke up the attack.

Shuttlesworth survived, and the violence had an unintended beneficial effect. As with the Little Rock Nine, who became heroes, Shuttlesworth's bravery won him groups of followers. The civil rights movement gained much-needed foot soldiers. African-American leaders needed people who were willing to go to jail. They needed people who were willing to risk their jobs, their homes, and even their lives.

But Shuttlesworth was already a well-known, active leader. Elizabeth Eckford was just a teenager who wanted a better education. She knew her famous picture moved millions of people, but for her, it didn't represent a moment of pride. It represented a moment of terror.

Decades after the conflict, she told a reporter: "One time I asked people to not put that picture in front of

African-American leaders needed people who were willing to go to jail. They needed people who were willing to risk their jobs, their homes, and even their lives.

Civil rights leader Fred Shuttlesworth survived several attempts on his life, including a bombing and being beaten with chains and brass knuckles in 1957.

Elizabeth Eckford and the statue depicting her, which the sculptor, John Deering, said is "looking ahead with a mix of stoicism and apprehension."

Pulitzer Prize-nominated photos by Will Counts provided the basis for the features of the life-size statues honoring the Little Rock Nine on the grounds of the Arkansas State Capitol.

my face. They didn't understand. They kept bringing that picture for me to sign. So what I do now is I keep some tissues and put it over the pictures as though I'm protecting it, while I sign the skirt."

Eckford is retired from her job as a probation officer in Little Rock. After high school she attended college in Ohio, and in 1967 joined the Army. After five years she moved back to Little Rock, where she has lived a quiet life ever since.

1957 Little Rock Nine   **37 USA**

2005

While Little Rock Central High School is now a national historic site, African-American leaders don't consider what happened there a turning point in school integration. The Little Rock conflict ended with a victory, but efforts to integrate schools in many parts of the country remain slow and controversial more than 50 years later. Lawmakers and judges still struggle with the issue, and the state of America's inner-city schools can be seen as evidence of racism in disguise.

But Melba Pattillo Beals, one of the Little Rock Nine, sees progress. And it gives her hope. Four decades after the conflict, she returned to Central High School and took a tour.

"When I got to the top of the stairs I saw a young black boy wearing wire-rimmed glasses, slight of stature. He bowed and said, 'Welcome to Central High School. I'm the president of the student body.' Of course, I was quite tearful. Climbing all those stairs, seeing him. I hadn't been up those stairs in 40 years.

"So when he stepped out, I was expecting something other than this black child. This had been my dream, my vision. This was why I had endured all the pain and physical punishment—so this boy could stand there and say that. It was amazing."

Timeline

U.S. Supreme Court's decision in *Plessy v. Ferguson* upholds "separate but equal" accommodations under Jim Crow laws

1896

May 1954

In *Brown v. Board of Education*, the Supreme Court rules that separate is *not* equal and segregation in public schools is unconstitutional; the Little Rock School Board says it will follow the Supreme Court's decision and integrate its schools

The Little Rock School Board approves a plan to gradually integrate its schools, beginning with high school in 1957; advocates for integration want the board to move faster, but a judge supports the board's plan

May 1955

September 23, 1957

A mob of more than 1,000 whites protests at Central High School while the nine African-American students enter through a side door; with the crowd threatening violence, police remove the nine students to keep them safe

September 24, 1957

President Dwight D. Eisenhower sends federal troops to Little Rock and federalizes the National Guard

August 1957

Segregationists hold public meetings to build opposition to the school board's plan

September 4, 1957

Governor Orval Faubus sends the National Guard to Central High School to prevent nine African-American students from entering the school; soldiers turn away 15-year-old Elizabeth Eckford, who arrives first, and the other eight

September 25, 1957

Troops escort the nine African-American students into Central High School for their first full day of classes

February 20, 1958

Following months of conflict at the school, the Little Rock School Board seeks the court's permission to delay integration

Timeline

May 27, 1958

Ernest Green becomes the first black student to graduate from Central High School

Summer 1958

A judge allows the school board to delay integration, but the U.S. Supreme Court orders the school board to continue with its plan to integrate schools; the school board decides to start school in September as planned, but Governor Faubus closes all the schools

Segregationist school board members are recalled and replaced with moderates

May 25, 1959

June 18, 1959

A court rules the school-closing law unconstitutional, and the school board announces schools will reopen in the fall

Little Rock residents vote overwhelmingly to stop integration; the city's public high schools are closed, and Little Rock students are forced to enroll in private schools, travel to schools outside the city, or take correspondence courses

September 27, 1958

December 6, 1958

A new school board is elected with members evenly divided between pro- and anti-integration

Moderate school board members walk out after segregationist members attempt to fire 44 teachers and administrators who favor integration

May 5, 1959

August 12, 1959

Little Rock public high schools reopen nearly a month early; Faubus tells segregationists that it is a "dark" day and they should not give up the struggle; segregationists march to Central High School to protest, but they're turned away by police; two of the Little Rock Nine return to Central for their senior year

Fall 1972

Fifteen years after the Little Rock Nine encountered an angry mob and armed guardsmen, Little Rock's public schools are fully integrated

Glossary

bigot—person who treats people of a different group with hatred

boycott—to refuse to do business with someone as a form of protest

correspondence courses—courses taken by students through the mail

desegregation—the process of ending the practice of separating groups of people by race in public places

federal government—the central government of the United States, consisting of the executive branch (the president), the legislative branch (Congress), and the judicial branch (the U.S. Supreme Court and other federal courts)

harass—to annoy, disturb, and pick on someone

neutral—not taking a position or showing an opinion

reconciliation—the act of coming together with understanding and forgiveness

Reconstruction—period following the Civil War, from 1865 to 1877, when the federal government governed states in the former Confederacy and granted rights to African-Americans

referendum—election in which citizens vote on a legislative question

segregation—practice of separating people of different races, income classes, or ethnic groups

Additional Resources

Further Reading

Beals, Melba Pattillo. *Warriors Don't Cry: A Searing Memoir of the Battle to Integrate Little Rock's Central High.* New York: Pocket Books, 1995.

Fitzgerald, Stephanie. *The Little Rock Nine: Struggle for Integration.* Minneapolis: Compass Point Books, 2007.

Jacoway, Elizabeth. *Turn Away Thy Son: Little Rock, The Crisis that Shocked a Nation.* New York: Free Press, 2007.

LaNier, Carlotta Walls, with Lisa Frazier Page. *A Mighty Long Way: My Journey to Justice at Little Rock Central High School.* New York: One World Ballantine Books, 2009.

Walker, Paul Robert. *Remember Little Rock: The Time, the People, the Stories.* Washington, D.C.: National Geographic, 2009.

Internet Sites

Use FactHound to find Internet sites related to this book. All of the sites on FactHound have been researched by our staff.

Here's all you do:
Visit *www.facthound.com*

Type in this code: 9780756544409

Source Notes

Page 4, lines 3 and 19: David Margolick. "Through a Lens, Darkly." *Vanity Fair*. 24 Sept. 2007. 24 March 2011. www.vanityfair.com/politics/features/2007/09/littlerock200709?currentPage=all

Page 5, line 6: Ibid.

Page 6, line 8: Ibid.

Page 6, caption: I. Wilmer Counts. *A Life Is More Than a Moment: The Desegregation of Little Rock's Central High.* Bloomington: Indiana University Press, 1999, p. 40.

Page 7, line 11: "Crisis in Little Rock." American Radio Works. 22 March 2011. http://american radioworks.publicradio.org/features/marshall/littlerock1.html

Page 7, line 25: Ibid.

Page 8, line 3: Gene Roberts and Hank Klibanoff. *The Race Beat. The Press, The Civil Rights Struggle, and the Awakening of a Nation.* New York: Alfred A. Knopf, 2007, p. 161.

Page 8, line 6: Ibid.

Page 8, line 10: Ibid.

Page 10, line 16: "Will Counts, 70; Noted for Little Rock Photo." *The New York Times.* 10 Oct. 2001. 22 March 2011. http://query.nytimes.com/gst/fullpage.html?res=9404E6DF1F3CF933A25753C1A9679C8B63

Page 15, line 4: "Thurgood Marshall, Civil Rights Hero, Dies at 84." *The New York Times.* 25 Jan. 1993. 24 March 2011. http://query.nytimes.com/gst/fullpage.html?res=9F0CEFD71639F936A15752C0A965958260&pagewanted=all

Page 15, line 13: "The Southern Manifesto." American Radio Works. 24 March 2011. http://americanradioworks.publicradio.org/features/marshall/manifesto.html

Page 15, line 29: Benjamin Fine. "Militia Sent to Little Rock; School Integration Put Off." *The New York Times.* 3 Sept. 1957. 24 March 2011. http://tv.nytimes.com/learning/general/specials/littlerock/090357ds-militia.html

Page 17, line 3: Black History. Biographies. Daisy Bates. 24 March 2011. www.gale.cengage.com/free_resources/bhm/bio/bates_d.htm

Page 19, line 10: Jane Emery. "Can You Meet the Challenge?" *The Tiger.* 19 Sept. 1957. 24 March 2011. www.ushistory.org/us/54c.asp

Page 22, line 3: "Eckford: Central High in 1957 'was not ... a normal environment.'" CNN. 17 May 2004. 24 March 2011. www.cnnstudentnews.cnn.com/2004/LAW/05/17/eckford.transcript/index.html

Page 22, line 10: "Clinton to hold door for 'Little Rock Nine.'" CNN. 25 Sept. 1997. 24 March 2011. www.cnn.com/US/9709/24/little.rock/

Page 23, line 5: Jefferson Thomas. 24 March 2011. www.america.gov/st/peopleplace-english/2010/September/20070821153542berehelleko. 9288446.html

Page 24, col. 2, line 15: Roy Reed. *Faubus: The Life and Times of an American Prodigal.* Fayetteville: University of Arkansas Press, 1997, p. 345.

Page 28, line 25: "Famed photographer had roots in area." *The Arkansas Leader.* 16 May 2007. 24 March 2011. www.arkansasleader.com/2007/05/from-publisher-famed-photographer-had.html

Page 31, line 3: "50th anniversary renews interest in Counts' photo." Indiana University School of Journalism. 11 Oct. 2007. 24 March 2011. http://journalism.indiana.edu/news/50th-anniversary-renews-interest-in-counts-photo/

Page 31, line 28: *A Life Is More Than a Moment: The Desegregation of Little Rock's Central High.* p. 57.

Page 32, line 5: "50th anniversary renews interest in Counts' photo."

Page 35, line 3: *A Life Is More Than a Moment: The Desegregation of Little Rock's Central High.* p. 41.

Page 36, line 9: David Margolick. "Through a Lens, Darkly."

Page 36, line 23: Ibid.

Page 37, line 5: "50th anniversary renews interest in Counts' photo."

Page 42, line 8: Civil Rights and the Press Symposium. Oral history interview with Dorothy Butler Gilliam. 24 April 2004. 24 March 2011. S.I. Newhouse School of Public Communications, Syracuse University. http://civilrightsandthepress.syr.edu/oral_histories.html

Page 44, line 9: Ibid. Oral history interview with Herb Kaplow.

Page 46, line 3: Kevin Sack. "On the 40th Anniversary of Little Rock Struggle, Clinton Warns Against Resegregation." *The New York Times.* 26 Sept. 1997. 24 March 2011. http://tv.nytimes.com/learning/general/specials/littlerock/0926little-rock.html

Page 50, line 27: Alex Chadwick. "One of the 'Little Rock Nine' Looks Back." NPR. 4 Sept. 2007. 24 March 2011. http://m.npr.org/news/front/14091050?singlePage=true

Page 52, caption: Kerry Kraus. "Impressive Sculpture Memorial Honors the Little Rock Nine." Arkansas Department of Parks and Tourism. 26 June 2007. 25 March 2011. www.arkansasmediaroom.com/news-releases/listings/display.aspx?id=860

Page 55, line 7: "Interview with Melba Pattillo Beals." Scholastic. 31 Jan. 1988. 24 March 2011. www2.scholastic.com/browse/article.jsp?id=4799

Select Bibliography

"A Historic Week of Civil Strife." *Life.* 7 Oct. 1957. 25 March 2011. http://books.google.com/books?id=ZFYE AAAAMBAJ&pg=PA48&dq=little+rock+nine&hl=en& ei=iMaMTaeRCoWitgf-t6WgDQ&sa=X&oi=book_resu lt&ct=result&resnum=3&ved=0CDUQ6AEwAg#v=one page&q=little%20rock%20nine&f=false

"Civil rights pioneer uses pain of past to send message today." CNN. 18 May 2004. http://articles.cnn. com/2004-05-17/justice/eckford.profile_1_black-students-white-students-elizabeth-eckford?_ s=PM:LAW

Counts, I. Wilmer. *A Life Is More Than a Moment: The Desegregation of Little Rock's Central High.* Bloomington: Indiana University Press, 1999.

"Crisis in Little Rock." American Radio Works. http:// american radioworks.publicradio.org/features/ marshall/littlerock1.html

The Encyclopedia of Arkansas History & Culture Project. www.encyclopediaofarkansas.net

Kirk, John A., ed. *An Epitaph for Little Rock: A Fiftieth Anniversary Retrospective on the Central High Crisis.* Fayetteville: University of Arkansas Press, 2008.

Kirk, John A. *Beyond Little Rock: The Origins and Legacies of the Central High Crisis.* Fayetteville: University of Arkansas Press, 2007.

Little Rock Central High School 40th Anniversary. www.centralhigh57.org

Margolick, David. "Through a Lens, Darkly." *Vanity Fair.* September 2007. www.vanityfair.com/politics/ features/2007/09/littlerock200709?currentPage=all

McWhorter, Diane. *Carry Me Home: Birmingham, Alabama: The Climactic Battle of the Civil Rights Revolution.* New York: Simon & Schuster, 2001.

Roberts, Gene, and Hank Klibanoff. *The Race Beat: The Press, The Civil Rights Struggle and the Awakening of a Nation.* New York: Alfred A. Knopf, 2006.

"Showdown in Little Rock." U.S. History.org. www.ushistory.org/us/54c.asp

Southern Oral History Program interview with Daisy Bates. 11 Oct. 1976. University of North Carolina at Chapel Hill. http://dc.lib.unc.edu/cdm4/item_viewer. php?CISOROOT=/sohp&CISOPTR=648&CISOBOX= 1&REC=1

Transcripts. Civil Rights and the Press Symposium. Oral history interviews. S.I. Newhouse School of Public Communications, Syracuse University. http:// civilrightsandthepress.syr.edu/oral_histories.html

Index